Spring is My Season

Photos and Story by
Robert J. Zimmer

"Spring is my season.
Spring is my time.
I sing and I dance.
I jump and I fly.

In spring, all is new.
In spring, there is new life
There is warmth and beauty
And colors so bright."

The Wild Geese

The wild goose returns to the place she calls home to raise a new family of goslings. All through spring, she watches over her babies, while Father stands guard.

"Honk, honk," says the wild goose,
"Spring is my time.
My children will learn
how to eat and to fly."

From the time they are hatched
The goslings can swim
They follow their parents
As summer begins

Spring is their season
The wild geese return
So much to teach
And so much to learn."

Even trees have flowers in spring.
These beautiful blossoms are the flowers of a red maple tree.

Flowers in the Forest

To walk in the spring forest is to see beauty and color in full bloom. Yellow, blue, white and pink flowers cover the forest floor, as the first bees and butterflies dance among the fresh blooms.

"Spring is their season,
Their colors so bright
Blue and purple,
Pink and white.

The warm spring sun touches the Earth
And the flowers begin to grow.
Waking from their long winter sleep
Beneath a blanket of snow."

"Spring is their season
Spring is their time
Flowers so pretty,
It is their time to shine."

Butterfly Wings

In the warm spring sun, butterflies take flight. You may see them on sunny days in April and May as they dance through the bare forest trees. Sometimes they hide to stay safe from predators. Can you spot the butterfly in this photograph?

Early in spring, there may be no flowers for butterflies to feed upon. This butterfly is feeding on sap from this tree.

The mourning cloak is always one of the first butterflies to appear in spring. At times, they may fly about when there is still snow on the ground.

Fox Snake

"Spring is my season," says the big fox snake.

Though large, this snake means no harm and keeps mouse numbers down. He is beautiful in yellow and dark brown with an orange head.

If you spot a large fox snake as you walk through the spring forest, keep a safe distance so he can crawl away peacefully.

Garter snakes also wake up in spring and come out of their winter shelters beneath the ground in large numbers.

A Chorus of Frogs

"Spring is my season.
We gather as one.
A chorus of frogs
Sings to the warm sun.

All through the day.
All through the night.
The frogs come together
To sing with all their might."

The Spring Peeper is one of our smallest frogs.
These are tree frogs and spend the summer among
the forest trees. They sing in spring with a high-
pitched "peep." Spring peepers often sing when there
is still snow on the ground.

The voice of the Green Frog sounds like a banjo string being plucked. The Green Frog is found along shorelines of ponds, lakes and marshes.

The song of the Leopard Frog sounds just like a loud, long snore.

"The leopard frog is spotted,
The green frog is not.
The tree frog changes colors
Depending upon his singing spot."

The toads sing loud in a spring chorus that can be heard a mile away. They float on the water or sing while perched along the pond edge.

The frogs and toads sing to find love. The females will lay their eggs which will soon become tadpoles during summer.

A Time for Turtles

"Spring is my season,"
The big snapping turtle says.
It is time for mother turtle
To leave the water and nest.

She walks slow and far
Leaving her wetland home
To find a perfect place
To dig her nesting hole.

She will lay her eggs, a dozen or more, deep in the
warm spring soil. Then, she will return to her pond
or marsh to spend the summer.

There are several types of turtles found in our area. The Snapping Turtle is the biggest. Don't get too close, her jaws are very powerful!

The rare Blanding's Turtle is black with gold spots and a bright yellow chin and throat.

The painted turtle is dark green or gray with red and yellow stripes. Here, she digs a hole with her hind feet, where she will lay her eggs.

All of these turtles leave their wetland homes for a short time each spring to nest in dry, sandy soil. As they do so, they face many dangers.

The biggest danger nesting turtles face is cars on roads and highways. Sometimes, turtles must cross our roads to reach their nesting spot. Cars going too fast on the road are the biggest danger.

Make sure your parents know to drive carefully and watch for turtles crossing roads and highways in spring.

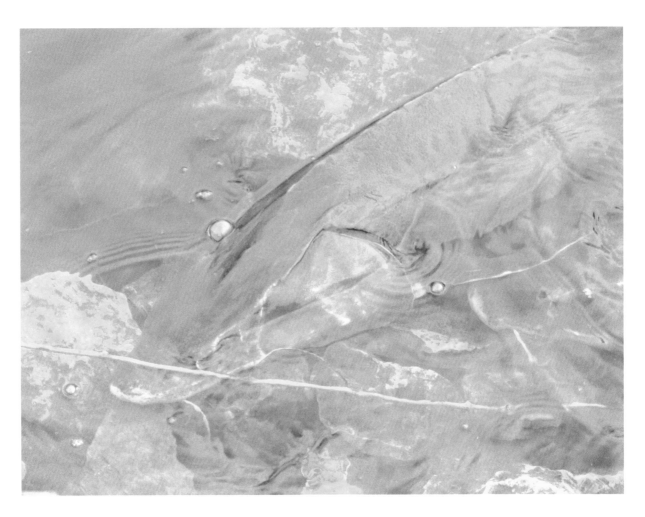

River Dance

The giant sturgeon swim miles up rivers to lay their eggs early each spring. These huge fish may be 6 feet long and weigh 200 pounds. They swim far to lay their tiny eggs along the rocky shore.

"Spring is my season.
I swim day and night.
I am on a long journey
When the rivers run high.

To the place I was born
I am now almost there.
Against the wild river,
A dance we will share.

My eggs fill the water
Clinging to the shore
New life will soon hatch
Like every year before.

I return down river
To my quiet water home.
To spend the summer in the shadows
I am never alone."

Spring of the Fawn

"Spring is my season,
Spring brings new life.
Hidden in the grasses,
Just out of sight."

The fawn remains quiet,
Silent and still.
While mother whitetail feeds
On the side of the hill.

Her baby is safe
He knows just where to hide
As quiet as a mouse
Everything is all right.

The Birds Return

"Spring is my season,
The season of birds
They return to their homes
To sing and be heard.

Colors so bright,
Voices so strong
They've returned here to nest
To the place they belong."

Ducklings can swim soon after they hatch. They swim together, learning how to feed from their parents during spring and early summer.

Young cranes are called "colts." They will stay with their parents throughout their first full year of life.

This beautiful bird is a Great Egret, our largest white heron. They quietly stalk shallow waters and wetlands looking for fish and frogs.

Great blue herons nest in groups, or colonies, in the treetops, feeding their young fish, frogs and other types of food until they are able to fly.

With a very long beak, the Woodcock is one of the strangest birds found here. He uses this long beak to probe into the ground looking for earthworms and other food. In spring, the Woodcock performs an amazing display dance and song at sunset.

"Spring is my season,"
The Chickadee says
Mom and dad work together
To create their new nest.

A hole in a stump
Or a log will do fine.
For spring is their season,
Their family time.

Mom and dad Chickadee work together to dig a nest hole, or cavity, in a rotting log or stump.

The American White Pelican also returns to Wisconsin lakes and wetlands to nest each spring. These birds nest on low islands in groups, or colonies.

"Spring is my season,
My season of life.
My season of hope,
A season so bright.

In spring, all is new
Journeys begin and they end
The wind carries us home
To start over again.

I sing and I dance,
My spirit so strong
My heart beats inside
I am where I belong."

21754439R00033

Made in the USA
Lexington, KY
11 December 2018